TELL ME ABOUT PIONEERS

SOJOURNER TRUTH

written by
John Malam

Evans

Evans Brothers Limited

Contact the Author

Tell me what you think about this book.
Write to the author at Evans Brothers.
Or e-mail him at: johnmalam@aol.com

VISIT OUR WEBSITE
www.evansbooks.co.uk

First published in paperback in 2007 by
Evans Brothers Limited
2A Portman Mansions
Chiltern Street
London W1U 6NR

Printed in China by WKT Company Limited

British Library Cataloguing in Publication data

Malam, John, 1957-
    Tell me about Sojourner Truth
    1.   Truth, Sojourner, d.1883 - Juvenile literature
    2.   African American women - Biography - Juvenile literature
    3.   Social reformers - United States - Biography - Juvenile
literature 4. Antislavery movements - United States -
History - 19th century - Juvenile literature
    I.   Title II.   Sojourner Ttuth
    306.3'62'092

ISBN-13: 9780237533618

SOJOURNER TRUTH

Acknowledgements

The author and publishers wish to thank The Local History Department, Willard Library, Battle Creek, Michigan, USA, for assisting in the development of this book.

Cover Peter Newark's American Pictures **Title page** Private Collection/Bridgeman Art Library **page 5** Historical Society of Battle Creek **page 6** Private Collection/Bridgeman Art Library **page 7** Corbis-Bettmann **page 8** Hirshhorn Museum, Washington D.C., USA/Bridgeman Art Library **page 9** Stapleton Collection, UK/Bridgeman Art Library **page 10** (left) Historical Society of Battle Creek **page 10/11** Private Collection/Bridgeman Art Library **page 12** Corbis-Bettmann **page 13** Peter Newark's American Pictures **page 14** (left) Peter Newark's American Pictures (right) Travel Ink/Ken Gibson **page 15** Peter Newark's American Pictures **page 16** Corbis **page 17** Historical Society of Battle Creek **page 18** (left) Historical Society of Battle Creek (right) Painting by James Watkins, by courtesy of the Historical Society of Battle Creek **page 19** (left) Historical Society of Battle Creek (right) Corbis-Bettmann **page 20** Historical Society of Battle Creek **page 21** Historical Society of Battle Creek

In America, about 200 years ago, a girl was born whose parents were slaves. They called her Isabella. Until she was thirty years old, Isabella was a slave too. She had many owners who made her work hard in their fields.

There came a time when Isabella was set free, and for the first time ever she could live life the way she wanted. She changed her name to Sojourner Truth, and she became a travelling preacher. She spoke about what she believed in. She spoke about the problem of slavery, about religion, and about women. People listened to her. This is her story.

This picture shows Sojourner Truth when she was about 60 years old.

Sojourner Truth's story really begins before she was born. It begins in Africa, where her parents came from. Her father was James, and her mother was Betsey.

James and Betsey were captured and sent across the sea to America. In America they were bought by a farmer. He was Johannes Hardenbergh. He wanted them to work on his farm in the little town of Hurley, which is in the state of New York.

Mr Hardenbergh owned other black Africans, too. They were all his slaves. He was their master. The slaves did whatever he told them to do.

Slaves were taken from Africa to America on ships like this. Many died on the long journey.

Mr Hardenbergh had moved to America from Holland. He spoke in Dutch, not in English. His slaves copied him, so they spoke Dutch, too.

James and Betsey had a daughter. They called her Isabella. Because her parents were slaves, Isabella was a slave from the day she was born. Like her parents, Isabella also belonged to Mr Hardenbergh.

Many slaves in America worked on the land. In the south of the country they picked cotton in their owners' fields.

Slaves were bought and sold at markets.

When Isabella was three years old, Johannes Hardenbergh died. His son, Charles, became her new owner. Isabella, her younger brother Peter, and her parents all went to live at Charles Hardenbergh's house. They lived in a damp cellar with his other slaves.

But when Charles Hardenbergh died, his slaves were sold to new owners. Isabella was taken from her family. She was only nine years old.

She was sold, with some sheep, to John Neely. Until then, Isabella had only spoken Dutch, like her first owners – but on Mr Neely's farm people spoke English. Mr Neely could not understand the little slave girl. He thought she was lazy, and he hit her.

When she was eleven, Mr Neely sold her to Martin Schryver. While she was with him she learned to speak English, but she never learned to read or write.

Many slave owners were cruel to their slaves.

When she was thirteen, Isabella was sold again. John Dumont paid £70 for her.

For sixteen years, Isabella worked on Mr Dumont's farm. While she was there, she married Thomas, another slave owned by Mr Dumont. Isabella and Thomas had five children.

Isabella learned that in some parts of America slaves were being set free. She wanted freedom from slavery more than anything else in the world.

Isabella's first child was Diana. Here she is when she was old. She looks like Isabella.

Mr Dumont promised to set Isabella free. But he broke his promise.

Isabella took her youngest daughter, Sophia, and ran away. She went to live with Isaac van Wagener.

Mr Dumont found out where they were. He told Mr van Wagener to send them back. But instead, Mr van Wagener gave Mr Dumont some money. It was enough to buy Isabella and Sophia their freedom. Isabella was thirty years old.

This painting shows slaves picking cotton.

Isabella found out that Mr Dumont had sold her five-year-old son, Peter. He had sold him to a man who lived outside the state of New York. This was against the law.

The law was on Isabella's side, and eventually Peter came back to her. Isabella was one of the first black people in America to use the law against a white man.

Even after slavery ended, families still lived in simple wooden cabins, like the one here. Isabella may have lived in a hut like this.

Isabella moved to New York City. She took Peter with her, but little Sophia was left behind with her older sisters on the Dumont farm. They would look after her.

Isabella found work as a cleaner. In her spare time she went to church. She joined a group of people who

sang hymns to the poor. But she wanted to do more for them, so she began to work with homeless women. She taught them how to cook and sew. Isabella hoped this would help them find work as servants.

Freed slaves often found work as servants.

One day, Isabella decided to leave New York City and travel the country. She wanted to start a new life for herself.

Isabella knew she was setting off on a long journey. She didn't know where she would go, or how long her journey would take. All she knew was that she wanted to tell people about her life. She wanted them to listen to her story. She wanted to make people see that slavery was a bad thing.

Isabella travelled on foot, and by horse and train.

The countryside through which Isabella travelled

Because Isabella was going to sojourn – this means 'to travel' – she changed her first name to Sojourner.

She also thought of a last name for herself. She called herself Truth. She felt God had told her to take this name.

Her name was now Sojourner Truth. Her new name matched her new life. She was a traveller who spoke only the truth.

Sojourner sold photographs of herself. She used the money to pay for her travels.

Women held meetings to discuss ways to fight for equal rights with men.

She travelled across America. Wherever she went she spoke to people about the evils of slavery.

She spoke about other things, too. She lived at a time when men thought they were superior to women. Sojourner believed this was wrong.

Sojourner was not afraid to speak her mind. She said that God had made all people equal, no matter if they were men or women, black or white.

Sojourner's book told the true story of her life. Many people read it. ▶

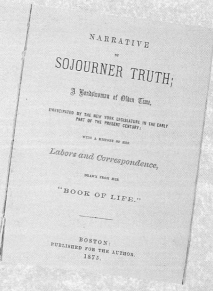

NARRATIVE
OF
SOJOURNER TRUTH;
A Bondswoman of Olden Time,

EMANCIPATED BY THE NEW YORK LEGISLATURE IN THE EARLY
PART OF THE PRESENT CENTURY;

WITH A HISTORY OF HER

Labors and Correspondence,

DRAWN FROM HER

"BOOK OF LIFE."

BOSTON:
PUBLISHED FOR THE AUTHOR.
1875.

Sojourner could not read or write. This is how she signed her name, when she was 83 years old. ▼

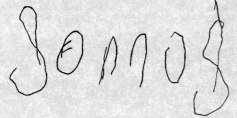

Sojourner was tall, and she usually wore a white scarf tied around her head. People noticed her straight away. She had a deep voice, and she could easily make herself heard.

She wanted more people to know what she had to say. But she could not read or write. She told the story of her life to her friend, Olive Gilbert, who wrote it down so it could be made into a book.

Posters told people when Sojourner was going to give a speech.

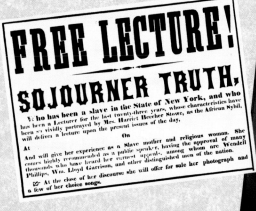

A modern painting of Sojourner, with the names of other people who have fought for human rights

Sojourner spoke at meetings. At one meeting a man said that women were weaker than men. Sojourner showed the crowd her arm. It was strong, like a man's, from her years working as a slave. This is part of what she then said:

"Ain't I a woman? I have ploughed, and planted, and worked as hard as any man, and eat as much, too. And ain't I a woman?"

18

When Sojourner was sixty she went to live in Battle Creek, a town in the state of Michigan.

In the 1860s there was a war in America. It was between the states in the north of the country and those in the south. The north wanted slavery to end. The south did not. During the war, the President of the United States, Abraham Lincoln, promised that slavery would end, and all slaves would be given their freedom.

The war in America was called the American Civil War.

Sojourner went to see President Lincoln to thank him for his promise to end slavery.

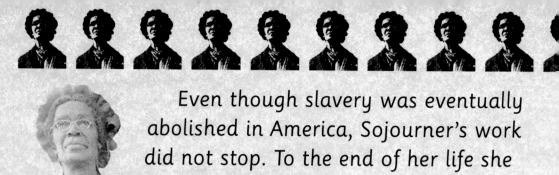

Even though slavery was eventually abolished in America, Sojourner's work did not stop. To the end of her life she spoke out against the many bad ways in which black people continued to be treated.

Sojourner Truth died in 1883. She was eighty-six years old. She is remembered today as a brave woman who fought for what she believed in. The good work she began has helped many people to live better lives today.

In 1999, a statue of Sojourner Truth was unveiled in Battle Creek, USA.

Important dates

c.1797 Isabella was born in Hurley, New York, USA

1800 Age 3 – her owner, Johannes Hardenbergh, died; his son, Charles, became her master

1806 Age 9 – she was sold to John Neely

1808 Age 11 – she was sold to Martin Schryver

1810 Age 13 – she was sold to John Dumont

1814 Age 17 – she married Thomas, also a slave

1826 Age 29 – she ran away to Isaac van Wagener

1827 Age 30 – she was freed from slavery

1828 Age 31 – she moved to New York City

1843 Age 46 – she changed her name to Sojourner Truth and became a travelling preacher

1850 Age 53 – the story of her life was published. It was called 'The Narrative of Sojourner Truth: A Northern Slave'

1851 Age 54 – she gave her "Ain't I a woman?" speech

1864 Age 67 – she met Abraham Lincoln

1865 All slaves in the United States were given their freedom

1883 Age 86 – she died in Battle Creek, Michigan, USA

A postage stamp was issued in 1986 in honour of Sojourner Truth.

Keywords

preacher
someone who believes in something, often to do with religion, and who speaks in public about it

slave
a person who is owned by someone else, and has to work for them

sojourn
to travel from place to place

state
the United States of America is divided into fifty parts, called states

Internet information
Find out more about Sojourner Truth:
http://www.sojournertruth.org/

Index